GW00854622

Section	Contents	Page

note from the author

I am a business person just like you.

My background is in management accounting. This means my focus is on providing businesspeople with current financial information about their business, which will help them make the right decisions for them. I also help with planning for the future so they are more likely to reach their goals.

I have worked with, and for, a wide range of different businesses in an extensive range of business areas.

This book is an attempt to capture what I have learned over the years. None of the ideas in this book are entirely original (as no business ideas ever are any more) so a big thank you to all the business people I have met over the years who have shared their expertise and experiences.

However, I hope the way the book is written will help you to better understand your business finances and enable you to capture information which will help you to make robust business decisions.

PRACTISING CERTIFICATE HOLDER

I am a Chartered Management Accountant (CIMA) and have more than 25 years' experience working in business.

Copyright © 2015 Bevan Financial Management Ltd.
All rights reserved. No part of this publication may be reproduced without prior permission of the author.

SECTION 1

UNDERSTANDING BUSINESS FINANCES

introduction - money talks

We all go into business to make money.

We may have a list of important and valid reasons why we choose to do what we do, and why running our own business helps us to achieve our goals - these reasons rarely revolve around money.

However, we cannot escape the fact that we need our businesses to make enough money for our individual circumstances. Any business which does not earn us a living is essentially a hobby – something we like to spend our time doing, but we need to do something else to put bread on the table.

It is vital, therefore, that you understand your business finances, and what drives your business's financial success.

Many business owners do not understand the financial position of their businesses, because they do not understand the terminology used by their accountants – and are often reluctant to ask.

This section is designed to help you understand the accounts you receive from your accountant so you can start to use this information to help you run your business.

focus

This section's focus is on understanding business finances and we're going to cover:

➜ How to make sense of what the profit and loss is telling you and how to apply it to your future business decisions

➜ The relationship between sales, margins and overheads

➜ The relationship between profit and cash

objectives

After completing this section you will be able to:

➜ Understand the financial position of your business from the reports your accountant or bookkeeper produces

➜ Use your financial information to make sound business decisions

➜ Understand why profit does not necessarily translate into cash in your bank account

profit or loss

an overview of profitability

The profit and loss statement is a financial document which should give you a clear picture of whether or not your business is making a profit, and how that profit is derived.

Profit and Loss Account

Marvin the Paranoid Android Industries

For the year ended 31st March X9

		X9		X8
		£		£
Turnover		50,000		45,000
Cost of Sales		(15,000)		(14,000)
Gross Profit		**35,000**		**31,000**
Overheads:				
Wages and Salaries	15,000		13,000	
Rent and Rates	2,000		2,000	
Utilities	1,500		1,000	
Motor and travel expenses	524		354	
Stationary, telephone, IT	2,230		1,687	
Bank charges and interest	45		37	
Subscriptions	650		450	
Insurance	1,500		1,650	
Marketing and Advertising	2,560		1,235	
Depreciation	2,500		2,100	
Total Overheads		28,509		20,413
NET PROFIT		**6,491**		**7,489**

quick guide to terms

Turnover – The total amount you have invoiced to customers

Cost of sales – The direct cost of what you sold, either in terms of materials or time, which varies with the quantity you have sold. Only include the costs of items that have specifically gone into producing what you have sold.

Gross Profit - Sales/Turnover less Cost of Sales

Overheads - The running costs, or fixed costs, you have to pay regardless of how much you sell.

Net Profit - Gross margin less overheads

detailed review

Sales/Turnover

The sales, or turnover line on the profit and loss statement is the one most business owners understand. It represents the money you have earned from selling your products/services.

However, most business owners only know the total sales they have made without any reference to which customers, or which products/services, have generated the income.

The benefits of having this knowledge are:

➜ If a large proportion of your sales are coming from one customer you will want to protect your business by selling more widely by expanding your customer base – this will reduce the risk to your business of this customer failing or going elsewhere.

  At the same time you will want to make sure you keep this customer happy as they are key to your current business success.

➜ If a large proportion of your sales come from delivering a particular product or service you need to acknowledge its importance to your business and ensure you continue to deliver to your customers' expectations.

In general you will want to focus future sales and marketing effort on those types of customers and products/services which work well for you now. In particular you will want to focus your effort on those sales that result in high margins.

Cost of Sales/Direct Costs

Cost of sales, or direct costs, are those costs which go directly into producing your products or services, and will fluctuate directly with your level of sales.

For example, if you are making a table the direct costs will be the wood you use, any incidentals such as screws, and the cost of the labour.

For a service company, direct costs might be employee wages, or subcontractor costs.

Gross Profit/Margin

Gross profit, or margin, is simply the difference between turnover and direct costs. It is important, therefore, that the direct costs incurred in producing a table, for example, are taken into account at the same time the sale of the table is. This is called cost matching. If you don't make sure the costs and the sale appear in the same period your financial reports will show wild swings in margin which are not representative of the real situation.

In service companies you will find the gross profit is generally a large percentage of sales. This is particularly true where the business owner is also the main service deliverer, because their pay will not be included in direct costs.

In contrast retail businesses will have a relatively lower gross profit, because much of the value of their offer is bought in, in the way of stock.

As with turnover, it is important you know the profit generated by each of your business's product/service areas.

You may find that much of the turnover generated by your business comes from products or services which make relatively little gross profit. If this is the case you may want to move your selling effort to higher margin products/services.

Overheads

'Overheads' is the general term used to describe those business costs which are 'fixed'. This means that, within reason, they remain the same irrespective of the level of sales.

Another important feature of overheads is that they only relate to types of individual expenditure which produce short term benefits for the company (i.e. less than 1 year). Land and buildings, motor vehicles, computers, furniture, as well as a company's intellectual property, can all be used by the company for many years – these are not overheads they are fixed assets (see below).

Overhead costs include:

- Wages and salaries (including yours)
- Rent and rates (including payments to you to compensate you for using your home as an office)
- Utilities
- Motor and travel expenses
- Professional fees
- Stationary, telephone and IT costs
- Bank charges and interest
- Networking and other subscriptions
- Insurance
- Marketing and advertising

If you understand your overhead expenses, and keep them under control, you can ensure every penny you spend contributes to the current, or future, goals of your business.

It is quite often useful to look at how much you will have to sell to enable you to spend in overheads.

Take the following example:

A joiner makes 25% gross margin on everything he sells. If he is going to make money he will have to make sure he sells at least £4 worth of goods for every £1 he spends on overheads.

Given that increasing sales is generally quite difficult, he may think twice about advertising in Yellow Pages, unless he is pretty confident the customers he wants to target use Yellow Pages to find suppliers.

One expense type many business owners struggle to understand is depreciation. It is derived from a balance sheet item called Fixed Assets and a full explanation is found on p14 below.

Net Profit

The profit you are left with once you have deducted all your day-to-day expenses.

profit v cash

turnover is vanity, profit is sanity, cash is reality

Whilst it is true that unprofitable businesses will have cash flow difficulties, it does not follow that profitable businesses will have cash in the bank.

There are several key reasons for this and these are found in the balance sheet.

The balance sheet shows what the business owns, is owed and owes at a specific point in time. The amount a business is owed and owes will affect the cash flow.

An example of a typical balance sheet is on the following page:

Balance Sheet

Marvin the Paranoid Android Industries

For the year ended 31st March X9

	X9		X8	
	£		£	
Fixed Assets		4,500		2,465
Current Assets:				
Stock	11,650		12,895	
Debtors	11,500		1,000	
Cash in Bank and in hand	4,560		(546)	
Current Liabilities:				
Trade Creditors	(14,985)		(5,580)	
Tax	(1,500)		(1,000)	
Net Current Assets		11,225		6,769
Net Assets		**15,725**		**9,234**
Capital and Reserves:				
Share Capital		100		100
Profit and Loss Account		15,625		9,134
Capital and Reserves		**15.725**		**9,234**

quick guide to terms

Fixed Assets – Items you buy for long term use in your business

Depreciation – The total amount included the profit and loss, for the use of fixed assets above (cost price divided by the number of years planned use in the business multiplied by the number of years it has been used in the business so far). The balance sheet is the *total* depreciation charged on assets, whilst the profit and loss shows the amount for just one year

Stock - Items bought for resale OR work done but not yet invoiced to the customer

Debtors - Unpaid customer invoices

Creditors - Unpaid supplier invoices

Capital/Reserves - Share capital and the money left in the company by you, the business owner, in the form of retained profit.

detailed review

Fixed assets and depreciation

Fixed assets are the type of business expense, which produce benefits for the business for more than one year.

Main types of fixed asset are:

* Land and buildings (including leases)
* Plant and equipment (factory/workshop machinery)
* Office equipment (computers and printers, telephone systems,
* Motor vehicles
* Intellectual property

Accountants deal with these items in a very particular way. If we included such high value items in the year in which they were purchased, profits would move up and down erratically year on year. This would make it difficult to see what the underlying profit of the business is. To avoid this problem the costs are instead spread over the years the asset is expected to be used in the business.

So, a motor car might be spread over five years, and each individual year would be charged with one fifth of the value as an expense called depreciation.

However, from a cash flow perspective fixed assets would go out in one hit, unless they were funded by HP or a loan.

This means a year when there were lots of fixed asset purchases might show a very poor cash flow even if profits are good.

Stock

We have already said that we want to match costs with the income they produce. However, sometimes a business will buy items, or do work, which will produce income in a subsequent period. This is known as stock or work in progress.

Although the business will get the sales, and payment from the customer, in the subsequent period, the stock may well have to be paid for earlier.

For example, in the case of a large project many hours of work might need to be done before the customer can be invoiced. This work might be spread over several months or years. All this work will be held in work in progress, so the profits of the company will not be impacted by the costs until the customer is invoiced.

However, throughout this time the company has to pay out wages and other costs. So its cash flow will be affected even if its profitability isn't.

Customers (Debtors)

When you look at your sales in a period you may expect your cash flow to improve by the same amount. However, any credit you give your customers will delay the benefit of these sales. The less credit you give the closer receipts into your bank will mirror sales you have achieved.

As you are not bankers by profession ask yourself why you are giving credit. If you are dealing with larger businesses, who will only buy from you if you offer credit, understand that you are taking the risk that they will pay slowly or, possibly, not at all. Are these risks you are prepared to take?

If dealing with smaller companies resist the temptation to give credit terms just because you think it is expected of you, and only give credit where there is a business case for doing so.

Suppliers (Creditors)

Conversely, any delay in paying suppliers will improve your cash flow.

A note of caution: use slow payment of suppliers judiciously. If you rely on suppliers to give you a good service don't jeopardise this relationship by delaying payment unfairly.

Bank loans and HP

By financing your business using loans and HP agreements you can mitigate the adverse cash flow effects of relatively large expenditure on fixed assets and other long term investments.

These are tools which should be used by companies with care. Both these instruments can be expensive and can be a drain on resources a long time into the future.

Never use a loan to finance working capital – i.e. a short term hole in your cash flow.

Tax

Most business owners forget about tax!

There are several key types of tax which affect any business (to find out more visit the HMRC website):

- There are forms of tax on employment. If you employ staff you will deduct PAYE and employees National Insurance from the employees' gross pay before you pay them.

  You have to pay this deducted tax to the Inland Revenue by 19th of the month following the relevant payroll. In addition you will need to pay employers' national insurance and the rate is currently 13.8%[1].

- VAT is a tax on goods and services and if your sales in a 12 month period exceed the VAT registration threshold you will need to add VAT at 20%[1] to all sales that fall within the scope of VAT. However, you can also reclaim VAT on purchases you have made where VAT has been added by the supplier.

- Corporation Tax is payable by all limited companies. The current corporation tax rate is 20%[1] charged on net profits and payable 9 months after the year end.

- If you are a sole trader (or a shareholder who is paid dividends) other taxes may be payable through your personal tax returns.

---

[1] Rates correct at time of publishing

An example of the timetable for the current tax year is below:

Tax year 6th April 2014 - 5th April 2015

Latest date to submit your tax return on line and pay any tax owing is 31st January 2016.

So remember whether you are a sole trader, partnership, or limited company, you will need to pay tax on the profits your business creates. Don't forget that at some point you will have to pay it!

starting to understand the figures

the four step plan

1. Look at your profit and loss

    Many business owners do not really look at the
    statements their accountants have prepared for
    them. Partly because the accounts are often
    pretty out of date by the time they are ready,
    but also because they don't understand what
    they are looking at.

    So step one is to start looking at your profit and
    loss reports and go back a few years so you can
    start to see trends in sales and costs.

2. Don't ignore the balance sheet

    As we have said there is a lot to be learned
    about the cash flow of the business by examining
    the balance sheet. For example, increasing stock
    and debtors will reduce your cash flow whilst
    increased creditors will increase it.

3. Ask tricky questions

    If there are areas of your accounts you don't
    understand ASK your accountant. Don't feel
    embarrassed because you think they will think
    you are daft for not having asked earlier.

    Remember they work for you – not the other way
    around.

4. Start to ask for more regular information.

learning and action steps

Don't forget to fill this section – it can make a real difference to how much you learn from the workbook and how useful it is in helping you master your business finances.

Actions I will start doing   Importance
   Date

Actions I will stop doing   Importance

Date

behaviour change log

Today's date _____

Review Date Issues	Reviewed	Outstanding
Tomorrow		
1 week		
1 month		
3 months		

SECTION 2

PATHETICALLY POOR PLANNING PRECEDES PALTRY PERFORMANCE

We all have goals in our lives which govern the decisions we make. Often, however, these goals remain unarticulated and unrecognised because we do not spend the time to really think where we want to go with our lives. Identifying our personal goals can, therefore, be a great starting point to understanding what we want to achieve.

Once we know what our goals are, we need to know that our business is going to deliver against them. Having a well-researched and thought through business plan can help by ensuring your business is on the right path.

Our business plan can then be put in monetary terms (a forecast) so we can measure our success, at regular intervals, in meeting the goals outlined in our plan.

Having a forecast is key to making the best out of the financial information provided to you by your bookkeeper/accountant because it puts the figures they produce into context.

business plans

introduction - what is a business plan?

For many small business owners a business plan is the document banks ask for when they are loaning the business money or extending an overdraft facility.

However, a business plan should be much more than that.

The reason banks like to see a business plan is that it gives them an indication that the business is under control and has clear goals. As the business owner you want that too. After all you would not build a house without a set of architect's plans.

A business plan should show you what your business will look like in the future and what actions you need to take to achieve the type of business you want. It is a vital tool in helping you identify your future strategies.

The beauty of going through the planning process is that you can ask yourself questions and find answers to potential problems BEFORE your business is impacted by them. You can also try out different scenarios on paper without risking your business.

focus

This section's focus is on building your business plan and we're going to cover:

→ How business planning can help you achieve your personal goals

→ What information you need to include in your business plan

objectives

After completing this section you will:

→ Be able to start down the journey of successful business planning

→ Know how to use your plan for decision making

clearing away the mental obstacles

Many business owners are reluctant to have a business plan. Key objections are often:

➔ I don't have time

As a business owner you have a responsibility to yourself to run your business rather than letting it run you. To do this you need to have a clearly thought through strategy. Your business plan is a great foundation on which to build your strategy.

You therefore need to make time to plan for your business's success.

➔ I don't have all the answers

No one has all the answers to the problems their business will encounter. However, having some advance warning of the problems which might arise, gives you a fighting chance of finding the solutions before they become critical. The business planning process often provides you with the answers to questions you had not yet thought of asking.

➔ I don't like writing documents

First and foremost your business plan is for your use. This means you can choose whatever format works for you. If you like having a feature length document fine, but other formats are just as valid. You could try using mind mapping, illustrations, photographs etc. The key points are that; your plan is down on paper, you are proud of it and you are happy revisit it.

➔ I don't have a crystal ball so I don't know what is going to happen in the future

None of us knows for certain what the future will bring but this should not stop us from planning. A business plan is based on what we want to happen and how we hope to achieve it. As the future becomes the present we can revisit our plans and tweak where necessary to account for our more accurate knowledge. The key thing is that our goals have probably not changed – just the path to getting them.

➔ I don't want a plan because I like to have flexibility

Having a well thought through plan can actually be liberating rather than restricting. If you know what your goals are you are more able to take advantages of opportunities which advance these goals. Uncertainty leads to inaction – your business plan helps to build certainty.

But often the real reason business owners don't write a plan, is that by writing a plan on paper involves a commitment to take defined actions. It is easier to let yourself off the hook if you don't make that commitment.

goals

Before you start building your business plan it is important you spend some time thinking about your personal goals and values. Here we are talking not just about your short term goals, but also your long term ones. Do you want your business to build into an asset you can sell? Should your business provide you enough income so you can have a great pension? Are there particular values you hold, which you want your business to be built around?

After all your business is only successful if it delivers against your personal criteria. If you have a clear idea what these are, you are in the best position to build a business plan, and therefore a business, which provides what you need.

what should be in your plan?

Your business plan should include anything pertinent to your business. Once it is written it should provide the clearest possible picture of where your business is now and how it will look in the future.

executive summary

Although the executive summary goes at the front of your plan it should be written last. As the name suggests it provides a summary of the business.

company description

It is useful to start your business plan with a review of what your company is about. You can include here:

- Your mission statement (if you have one)
- Your company ethos
- Your aims/goals
- Your team

  Although you may work on your own you may have strategic business partners you consider key to your business. If this is so it is worth acknowledging their importance to you and your business and including them in your team.

the offer

It is useful to be very clear on what your offer consists of. What are your key products/services and how do they solve your customers' problems.

the market

Your market

Having as clear a picture of the market your business operates in is the best way of ensuring your offer meets the needs of that market. By specialising you are most likely to be successful in matching your offer to customers who will value your product/service, so understanding the market will enable you to find your niche.

Your customers

For your business plan to be a true reflection of your business it is very important that you talk to your customers. You need to ask them about what you provide for them and the problems you solve.

This will help you in a number of ways:

- You will find out what really works for your customers
- You will know what to sell to future prospects
- It will help you find your niche

The competition

However unique you believe your product/service is there is always competition out there. If you are clear where that competition is coming from, you are best able to fight, avoid or pre-empt it.

SWOT analysis

Doing a SWOT is a great way of really opening up your business to scrutiny.

It is worth saying here that strengths and weaknesses tend to be internal to the business, whilst opportunities and threats come from external influences.

➜ Strengths

The strengths of your business will give you your competitive advantage. They should include any element of your business you perceive as being important to its success. You should include your personal strengths here because, as the business owner, your strengths are your business's strengths.

It sometimes difficult to identify what our real strengths are. If it helps as the people around you what they think your strengths are.

➜ Weaknesses

The weaknesses in your business will hold it back. However, if you know what they are, you are in a position to do something about them. Again, you should include your personal weaknesses here.

Clearly expressed weaknesses are difficult to ignore, so you are much more likely to take action if you are honest with yourself about what needs to change.

→ Opportunities

You should identify current possibilities offered by the market, which you have not yet exploited.

Opportunities can also come in the form of future changes in the market/economy which, if taken advantage of, will advance your business.

→ Threats

Your business may be affected by problems, either internally or externally generated, which need to be tackled now in order to protect its future.

Threats may also present themselves in the form of future changes in the market/economy which, if not addressed, will damage your business's future.

Interestingly an opportunity ignored can become a threat if your competition takes advantage of it.

You can use this page to start drawing up your SWOT analysis:

Strengths	Weaknesses
Opportunities	Threats

Your marketing plan

Your marketing plan should clearly present the strategy you are going to employ to market your offering to your chosen niche. You should then have a mechanism for measuring how effective your execution is.

It is a good idea to break your plan into short term and long term initiatives.

operations

Once you have looked at your goals and strategies you need to investigate how you are going to achieve them.

This part of the business plan clearly lays out HOW you do, or are going to do, what you do. It should show exactly how you deliver your product/service to your customers on a day to day basis.

You should also include key operational objectives for the coming year.

It is important you look at all the 'departments' of your business, what they need to do to 'deliver' for your business and how they will do it.

You should consider:

- Marketing

- Sales

- Finance

- Customer delivery

- Complaints

- Strategy creation/leadership

- Training

- Personnel

- Purchasing

- Admin

financials

Once you have got to this stage you will have a very clear idea of what your business looks and feels like. It is now time to put this information into monetary terms so you can review your business finances.

However difficult it might be, it is important that you forecast the sales and costs you believe will result from all the activities detailed above.

You also need to think about, and include, any larger equipment you will need to purchase.

planning effectively

the four step plan

1. Be clear on your goals

    It is much easier to plan effectively if you are clear on your goals – both personal and business. As Stephen Covey says, if you "start with the end in mind" you are more likely to be motivated by the journey.

2. Know your market

    Find out as much about the market you are operating in as possible. Every business owner should do the exercise regularly of assessing their business's place in the market in which they are competing. For planning purposes this knowledge is essential.

3. Be clear what your business is

    This does not just mean knowing what your business provides to its customers, but also understanding the full range of stake holders who affect the prosperity of your business, and whose prosperity is affected by it.

4. SWOT your business thoroughly

    A SWOT analysis can be a very helpful tool in assessing your business but it must be done thoroughly and honestly.

learning and action steps

Don't forget to fill this section – it can make a real difference to how much you learn from the workbook and how useful it is in helping you master your business finances.

Actions I will start doing   Importance Date

Actions I will stop doing   Importance Date

behaviour change log

Today's date _____

Review Date Issues	Reviewed	Outstanding
Tomorrow		
1 week		
1 month		
3 months		

forecasting for profit

introduction – forecasting effectively

Having a robust forecast can be an invaluable tool in managing your business finances. If done thoroughly it can show where deficits in cash flow may occur and give you a clear picture of the profits you may earn if your sales strategy is successful.

As well as reviewing the next 12 months you may want to include broad brush forecasts for up to five years.

As with any business planning tool it is important that it is reviewed as more up-to-date information is available. This will give you more accuracy when looking at expected future results.

Although there are specially written forecasting tools, a spreadsheet is all you need to get started.

An effective forecast will include both profit and loss and cash flow projections.

focus

This session's focus is on how to build up a picture of your future financial position and we're going to cover:

➔ What information you need to forecast effectively

➔ How to build a financial forecast

➔ How to use the forecast information

objectives

After completing this section you will:

➔ Be able to build a financial forecast for your business

➔ Know how to use your forecast for decision making

profit and loss

However difficult it might be, it is important that you forecast the sales and costs you believe will result from all the activities you will undertake in the coming year.

For each month try to predict as closely as possible what your sales and costs will be. Don't forget to include your salary. The timing of some items may be difficult to predict so it may be better to spread the total spend on these items evenly over the year.

If you use the same reporting format to forecast your profit and loss and your actual profit you will find it easy to compare your predictions with actual results.

See example of profit and loss on next page:

Profit and Loss Account

Marvin the Paranoid Android Industries

Forecast for the year ended 31st March X10

	Jan	Feb	Mar
	£	£	£
Turnover	5,000	6,000	4,000
Cost of Sales	(1,500)	(2,000)	(1,200)
Gross Profit	**3,500**	**4,000**	**2,800**
Overheads:			
Wages and Salaries	1,000	1,000	1,000
Rent and Rates	500	500	500
Utilities	100	100	100
Motor and travel expenses	50	50	250
Stationary, telephone, IT	250	250	850
Bank charges and interest	5	5	5
Subscriptions	650	0	0
Marketing and Advertising	1,000	200	250
Depreciation	250	250	250
Total Overheads	3,805	2,355	3,205
NET PROFIT	**(305)**	**1,645**	**(405)**
CUMULATIVE PROFIT	**(305)**	**1,340**	**935**	. . .

sales

Although none of us have a crystal ball there are ways you can approximate the level of sales you think you will achieve.

By having a separate line for each type of sale (whether you are breaking down by contract, customer or product area) you may well find it easier to picture where your sales are coming from.

Make sure you include any price increases you plan and allow for new customers, contracts or products. Caution: be realistic about these and explore how changes in new sales sources will impact on the whole model.

It is also worth splitting your turnover derived from repeat business from new business sales. This will help you to focus on what you need to achieve from your marketing spend in the year.

cost of sales

As you have split your sales into different line items it is advisable to split the cost of sales on the same basis.

overheads

Overheads can be relatively easy to predict if you make sure you have a clear idea of your current spend.

Again, you may find it easier to break down expenditure further - especially if the total is quite large. It also makes it easier to understand how the totals are derived. For example, the £1,000 marketing costs in January might be broken down into £500 for website revamp, £150 for networking and £350 for an advert in the local paper.

Wages and salaries

Your salary should be included here so make sure you have a realistic view of what you need to earn in the current year. If you pay yourself in the form of drawings (which do not normally appear in a profit and loss statement) still include them here. Likewise include predicted dividend payments if you use them as your chief form of income.

As with sales have a separate line per employee and total them to give the total wages and salaries.

Remember to include Employer's National Insurance on top of the gross salary per person.

If you are looking to take on staff, in addition to any current employees, make sure you include them from the date you expect their employment to start.

Rent and rates

Your rental agreement should lay out your financial commitments to your landlord along with when any rental increases will kick in.

Business rates will increase year on year so even if you don't know the exact level of future rate payments, it is wise to build in a percentage rise.

If you work from home make sure you include the costs of running the office (telephone, broadband, electricity etc.) from your house.

Utilities

Gas, electricity and water will also increase year on year but are more difficult to predict than rates. It is better to err on the side of caution and over state any price rise.

Motor expenses

Unless you expect your mileage to increase dramatically over the coming year, you should be able to use current levels as the basis for your forecast. Inland Revenue accepted mileage rates change very infrequently so continue to use the current rates (45p per mile for the first 10,000 miles, 10p per mile thereafter[1]).

If you use your actual motor expenses rather than mileage you may wish to allow for increasing petrol/diesel prices.

---

[1] Rates correct at time of publishing

Travel, office, bank expenses

Monthly variances in expenditure for these categories can be difficult to predict, so you may find it easiest to take your annual expenditure and divide it into 12 equal amounts.

However, do not forget to include any overdraft renewal fees, or loan arrangement fees, in the months they will be charged.

Networking

Networking costs will be split between annual subscriptions to the individual groups you use, regular costs for meals at meetings and ad hoc meetings with customers and 121s.

You should know when subscriptions are due and be able to include them in the correct month. For meal and ad hoc meeting costs, it may be easiest to predict the annual cost and split into 12 equal amounts.

Professional fees

Professional fees often come in large one-off expenditure, unless you have an accountant who breaks their fixed fee into monthly payments. You should have a clear idea from you past year's experiences when these fees will be payable.

Subscriptions and training

Don't forget to include your personal development costs in terms of subscriptions to trade organisations and training.

Marketing and advertising

Here you should include the costs of any specific marketing initiatives, advertising campaigns, web site development and maintenance, or general expenditure on business cards, leaflets or other promotional material.

Depreciation

You should know the monthly depreciation on existing assets – it will simply be the annual depreciation divided by 12. To this add depreciation on new assets you plan to purchase during the year.

cash flow

Once you have prepared your month by month profit and loss forecast, you can then look at how your cash flow might look.

Cash flow

Marvin the Paranoid Android Industries

Forecast for the year ended 31st March X10

	Jan £	Feb £	Mar £
Opening bank balance	475	2,336	(1,753)
Receipts:			
Sales	6,250	5,750	6,900
Payments:			
Cost of sales purchases	1,725	1,725	1,955
Wages and Salaries	1,000	1,000	1,000
Rent and Rates	500	500	500
Utilities	115	115	115
Motor and travel expenses	57	57	287
Stationary, telephone, IT	287	287	997
Bank charges and interest	5	5	5
Subscriptions	650	0	0
Marketing and Advertising	50	1,150	230
Purchase of van	0	5,000	0
VAT			765
Total Payments	4,389	9,839	5,854
Net cash flow	1,861	(4,089)	1,046
Closing bank balance	2,336	(1,753)	(707) ...

There will be a number of items which appear on the profit and loss but do not affect cash flow, and vice versa. There are also items which will appear with different values:

VAT

The figures on your profit and loss should not include VAT (unless you are not registered for VAT in which case irrecoverable VAT will be included in costs). However, your payments and receipts will include VAT (where applicable) and so your cash flow will show the VAT inclusive amount.

Every three months or so you need to budget to pay/reclaim any VAT owed.

Sales

Any delay in your customers paying your invoices will affect your cash flow. You may find receipts lag sales by a month or two. Conversely, if you collect deposits from your customers you may find your receipts precede sales.

Purchases/overheads

If you are buying in items for resale, you may well pay for these goods earlier than you sell them on. In this case the costs will appear in the cash flow before they appear on your profit and loss – remember the matching principle.

Also, even if you incur the costs at the same time as you invoice the customer, there will be a lag if you take advantage of credit terms from your suppliers.

Fixed assets

Any fixed assets bought in the period will have a direct impact on cash flow, unless financing is used to fund their purchase.

Conversely, depreciation in the profit and loss will not impact on cash flow.

making your financial forecast part of your decision making process

By the time you have completed your financial forecast, you will have reviewed your plans for the coming year in a very detailed manner.

It makes sense to use this information to make effective decisions.

For example, you will have a clear idea of the profit you can achieve given the spending you predict. Even if you spend your marketing 'budget' on a different mix of initiatives, as long as the total does not exceed the amount in the forecast, you will not see a change in the overall profit. This can give you the freedom to make decisions on opportunities which present themselves.

Similarly, the cash flow forecast gives you an idea of the peaks and troughs in cash flow your business may experience. You can use this information when you are planning key purchases. If you have flexibility in when you make the purchase, it makes sense to do so when there is cash in the business. If you cannot match the purchase to cash availability, you know in advance that you will need to use your overdraft facility, or find funding.

The ability to plan ahead can be invaluable in making your business as financially stable as possible.

Finally, make sure you update your forecast regularly for changes in circumstances. For larger businesses it may be necessary to do monthly updates, whilst for smaller ones quarterly should be enough (as long as there are no big changes in circumstances).

forecasting effectively

the four step plan

1. Understand where your business is now

   Before you even think about forecasting for the future it is important you understand the current financial position of your business and what drives the results.

2. Instead of focussing on the money focus on what it represents

   It is easier to put together a forecast if you think of what the money represents. For example, if you are forecasting your monthly wages bill, first identify which people should be included, and only after you have done that assign a cost to each person.

3. Forecast for cash flow not just profit

   The most useful part of any forecast is the cash flow it generates. This will tell you if further funding is needed or if you can afford to pay yourself the income you need out of the profits the business makes.

4. Get help if you need it

   Financial forecasting is difficult and getting it wrong can lead you to make the wrong decisions – or prevent you from getting the funding you need. So if you are not sure what you are doing we urge you to get professional help.

learning and action steps

Don't forget to fill this section – it can make a real difference to how much you learn from the workbook and how useful it is in helping you master your business finances.

Actions I will start doing   Importance   Date

Actions I will stop doing   Importance   Date

behaviour change log

Today's date _____

Review Date Issues	Reviewed	Outstanding
Tomorrow		
1 week		
1 month		
3 months		

SECTION 3

NEITHER A BORROWER NOR A LENDER BE?

FINANCING YOUR BUSINESS

One of the most common problems in businesses of all sizes is how to find finance.

This section is all about this issue and gives you the basic understanding you need to finance your business effectively.

We will cover the different types of financing available to you – some of which may be surprising.

The best way of financing your business is through making profits, which turn into cash. A key way to be profitable is to make sure you charge the 'right' rate to your customers so we will start with pricing effectively.

Although pricing will help move you in the right direction it will only help your cash flow if you are effective in invoicing and collecting outstanding money from your customers.

Finally, there are the ways you can obtain financing from third party providers, which we will also be examining.

pricing effectively

introduction – choosing the right price

Getting your pricing right is the key to building a profitable business. Charge too little and you will go out of business because you cannot pay the bills. Charge too much and you will go out of business because you won't sell anything.

The price you can command for your product or service is governed by factors both inside and outside your control, so you need to fully understand the value of what you supply to your customers.

How you choose to price your product/service will tell customers more about what to expect than just what they are being asked to pay - so pricing can be a mine field from more than one stand point.

focus

This section's focus is on pricing and we're going to cover:

➜ The problems business have with pricing
➜ Gathering the right information to price correctly
➜ How to price your product/service confidently

objectives

After completing this section you will be able to:

➜ Identify your value proposition
➜ Be able to price confidently
➜ Move towards building a profitable business through a clear pricing strategy

the pricing problem!

confidence

Confidence affects everything about your business not least your ability to price your product/service effectively. It is important to get to grips with:

What value you are giving your customers

Too few business owners understand the real value their customers get from using their product/service. If you can't define your value you will not be able to price effectively.

What your product or service is

Many businesses, particularly in the service sector, are not clear on exactly what their customers are paying for. This leads to discrepancies in service delivery and real problems with billing.

the market

You do not run your business insulated from market conditions – you are surrounded by other companies vying to attract the attention of your customers, and potential customers. So, make sure you are you clear on:

Who your competitors are

Customers will compare the value of your product/service against that of your competitors. If you don't know enough about your competitors' products/services you will have a problem demonstrating your value offering.

What other products/services you are competing against

Even if you think your product/service is 'unique' you will still be competing with other companies for customers' spending power, or with different solutions which solve the same customer problem. Unless you understand your position in the market, you won't be able to demonstrate why spending with your businesses is the most effective use of the customers hard earned pennies - so market research is key.

Financial knowledge

Unfortunately far too few small businesses owners are on top of their business finances. If you wait for your annual accounts to help you make financial decisions your information will be way out of date. It is vital you use up to date financial information when putting your pricing together. Particularly you need to know:

- What the full costs are in your business

  For any business to flourish it must take more money in than it expends out. It is as simple as that. However, if you don't know your business expenditure clearly enough you will not know the minimum you need to earn to make a profit. This means you will have no minimum price point.

- What your pricing strategy is

  Because reviewing prices is a difficult job many business owners avoid doing it on a regular basis. This means when they do put up their prices, they have to make large increases which customers find hard to take.

- What equipment you need to buy in the coming year and how much it will cost

  As well as understanding your daily running costs it is also important you know what you are likely to need in the form of largish investments. Will you need new computers, machinery, a car...? If so, you need to ensure your business brings in enough money to pay for these too.

factors to think about

value

The most effective way to price is to establish what the value of your product/service is to your customers. This value is defined by the following:

➜ Your exact product or service - clearly defined

➜ The 'perceived' value of that product/service to the customer, which will be a function of:

- How much the customer needs or wants it

- What else is in the market place to fulfil that need or want

➜ The customers perception of your business and the quality of your offer

➜ The customers' perception of your competition

➜ What else the customer could spend their money on

The only way you can really understand your customers' needs and wants is to do your research.

Look at the elements of what you do that differentiate you from your competitors. Talk to your customers and find out why they buy from you – this will give you the confidence to recognise your own value. Make it very clear to customers the full value they get from your product/service – based on what they need and the problems you solve – and move the discussion away from pricing. That way it is more difficult for customers to make a direct comparison with competitors and makes them less likely to buy purely based on price. Even if you run a shop you can differentiate yourself based on the level of service you give your customers.

If you are struggling to put a price on what you do, look at what the 'market value' of your product/service is. A way of finding this out is to look at what your direct competitors are charging for the same element of value. It is very important that you compare like with like. So for example a handmade kitchen does not have the same value as a B&Q kitchen even if the basic elements are the same.

more about perception

As indicated above one of the most important lessons you can learn is that creating value in your business is all about your clients' perception.

You can change the perceived value of your product/service by changing the way your business is presented. A brand new porcelain dish sold at a car boot sale will command a far lower price than the exact same dish sold at Harrods. This is not because the dish sold at Harrods is any better but because the customers' *perception* of the value of the dish is altered due to the way it has been presented for sale.

Another interesting thing to note is that price can influence the customers' perception of quality. When presented with a price they believe is too low, customers may suspect the product/service is of poor quality. Alternatively, some companies publicise their product as being 'reassuringly expensive' thus emphasising that quality generally comes at a cost.

costing

So, you know how much your customers are prepared to pay for what you provide, but is it enough to make you money?

To answer this question you need to have enough financial information about your business to fill in the following formula:

PROFIT = TOTAL REVENUE – TOTAL COSTS

Where:

TOTAL REVENUE = price **x** quantity sold

TOTAL COSTS = costs directly involved in providing goods and services **+** monthly overheads **+** your salary

If the revenue you will earn by charging the market price is less than your total costs, you will not make money!

Your options then are to increase the volume of what you are selling, or to reduce costs.

If you don't know what the costs of running your business are FIND OUT!

Although it is difficult to estimate the volume of products/services you may sell in the coming year, it is important to estimate what you are likely to achieve. No one has a crystal ball and initially your forecasted activity may be wrong. However, if you build a clear picture of what you are achieving, your ability to forecast will become more accurate. (See the forecasting section for more help).

hourly rates

If you are in the service sector you may be interested in knowing what hourly rate to apply – even if you are charging on a fixed fee basis, you may want to have a notional hourly rate to use when working out what the fixed fee should be.

> HOURLY RATE =
>
> Total cost of running your business
> **DIVIDED BY**
> Total number of chargeable hours

The total costs of running your business will be as previously defined. The total number of chargeable hours can be difficult to calculate but it is important you try to get as accurate a figure as possible – it is likely to be lower than you think. Note: chargeable hours are those hours the customer is directly paying for.

Essentially the calculation is:

> TOTAL NUMBER OF CHARGEABLE HOURS =
>
> 52 Weeks **x** 5 days **x** hours in the working day
> **less** holidays (in hours)
> **less** time spent on non-chargeable activities

resistance to increased pricing

To make increasing your prices easier, and to avoid customer resistance, make small increases each year.

Many companies will use 1st January as a good date on which to regularly increase prices. If customers know this is your policy they are less likely to object because they know it is coming. You can then increase prices easily by 1-5% - an amount most customers find acceptable. At the very least you can increase your prices by the level of inflation.

A relatively small price increase each year makes a big difference to the level of profitability in your business.

pricing with confidence

the four step plan

1. Know your competition

   Identify key competitors and find out how much they charge. Don't just concentrate on competitors who have the same product or service, but also look at who you might be competing with for customer spend.

2. Establish value

   Once you have a good idea what the market value of your product or service is you can be more confident that your prices are realistic.

   If you are charging much less than the market price PUT YOUR PRICES UP!! However, make sure you talk to your customers throughout the process to keep them on board.

   If you are charging more than the market value this may well be a hindrance to increasing volume UNLESS you have established a recognised higher level of value than your competitors - in which case this is great!

3. Forecast

   Do a financial forecast so you are clear of your business expenses – if you need help with this your accountant should be able to help.

This will enable you to make sure you are making a profit at the price level you want to set, with the volume of sales you believe this price will achieve.

4. Review regularly

   Set a regular time each year when you will review your prices – and keep to it!!!

learning and action steps

Don't forget to fill this section – it can make a real difference to how much you learn from the workbook and how useful it is in helping you master your business finances.

Actions I will start doing   Importance Date

Actions I will stop doing   Importance Date

behaviour change log

Today's date _____

Review Date   Reviewed   Outstanding
Issues

Tomorrow

1 week

1 month

3 months

debt collection

introduction – collecting what is owed to you

Collecting the money owed to them by customers is a difficult exercise for many businesses.

However, many of the problems are created by the businesses themselves because they don't have a well thought through system for invoicing and then asking for the money owed.

If you invoice late and then just wait for the money to come in from customers, you are likely to be waiting a long time. Most customers will pay those businesses that chase for money first – it is just human nature.

Good customers of yours will understand that prompt payment is necessary for you to run your business effectively and will often just need to be prompted into paying.

This section is all about how you can make it as easy as possible to overcome the debt collection hurdle.

focus

This section's focus is on collecting what is owed to you and we're going to cover:

➜ How important invoicing effectively is to your cash flow

➜ How to make sure your customers know what to expect

➜ How to collect money once it is owed

objectives

After completing this section you will be able to:

➜ Invoice effectively

➜ Collect money from the vast majority of customers in a timely manner

➜ Know how to approach customers who are not paying

why effective invoicing is key

It may seem obvious but collecting money from your customers is absolutely vital to the financial health of your business.

After all you are in business because you provide a product/service customers want to buy. It goes without saying that these customers will expect to pay you for what you provide.

However, unless you are invoicing effectively you will not be giving your customers the opportunity to pay you promptly!

how to ask your customers for money

don't assume every customer can pay

Just because a client has given you an order for goods and services does not mean they have the cash to pay you.

In tough economic times, in particular, businesses may be on the verge of bankruptcy for some time before they actually go under. During that period suppliers can be left waiting for a long time for their money – if they are lucky enough to get paid at all.

To protect your business it makes sense to find out as much about a prospective customer's finances as you can. There are various credit agencies that can provide financial reports and even free sites such as DueDil.co.uk can help.

A word of caution though – don't just take a credit report at face value as they are not always accurate.

You can also ask around about the customer – particularly if they are local to you – and see how they pay other suppliers.

It is also worth running regular credit checks on existing customers who generally owe you large sums of money – especially if they start drawing payment out.

If you are worried about a customer's credit worthiness DO NOT GIVE CREDIT.

tell your customers at the outset how you will behave

Many businesses do not have the process in place to inform their customers what their procedure for collecting money is.

The vehicle for doing so is the sales order/letter of engagement with your terms of business and it is good practise to send one out when a customer places an order.

The sales order should give the following information:

➔ Confirmation of what exactly has been ordered (this applies equally to services as well as goods)

➔ Confirmation of when the order will be fulfilled

➔ The agreed price

➔ At what point you will invoice.

This should be as soon as possible after the delivery of the goods and services. Where the service is delivered over multiple months it is good practise to invoice evenly over these months so that you are paid evenly rather than in a lump sum at the end.

➔ What your payment terms are.

Many businesses give credit without giving any thought to why they are doing so. There is a myth that all businesses should give credit but this is not so. Only give credit when there is a commercial reason for doing so.

If you do give credit, give proper consideration to how long you will give customers to pay and make sure this is clearly displayed on the sales order, invoices and debt collection correspondence.

THEN STICK TO IT.

→ Make sure you tell clients clearly in your terms of business what the consequences are of not paying on time.

This is not being aggressive it is just being professional.

invoice as soon as you can

As you have told your customers what to expect make sure you invoice as your terms of business lay out.

The date you invoice your customers is key in getting paid promptly and will be the point the clock starts ticking. So the sooner you invoice the sooner you will be paid.

Some business owners are their own worst enemy because they don't have the procedures in place to ensure customers are invoiced promptly.

For example, many electricians who quote their customers a fixed price for doing work do not have invoices ready prepared for their customers before they leave the job. Having an invoice to hand will make it more likely the customer will pay there and then, whilst you are on the premises, rather than paying later when they remember.

Invoicing promptly is not only a professional way to behave but also helps customers pay you quickly.

keep an eye on outstanding debts and start chasing in line with your policy

If you don't have a way of getting regular information about outstanding debtors it is well worth finding out how you can get this information quickly and easily. (See the section on developing your information systems).

You should then monitor the situation regularly so no debts get too old.

It is worth having a couple of standard chasing emails/letters that can be sent out at predetermined dates after invoices become due.

The first letter should be a general chasing letter requesting payment and should be sent out immediately payment is due – this may be sent out with a statement which clearly gives the details of the invoices outstanding.

If you have not received payment within two weeks of the first letter going out it may be a good idea to phone the customer – see the debt collection conversation below for an idea how to handle that call.

A second letter detailing your terms of business and indicating interest may now be applied to those invoices still outstanding, should probably be sent out within a month of the invoices becoming overdue. The exact text of this letter may depend on how the call to the customer, above, went. Don't send a second letter to customers who have agreed to put you in their payment run unless the customer defaults on the promised payment.

debt collection conversation

Debt collection conversations with customers can be tricky but are most likely to get the required result if you are prepared. Below is an example of how to handle the call.

If you are reluctant to call your customer yourself it may be a good idea to employ your bookkeeper to do the phone calls for you.

preparation

Make sure you have the name of the correct person to speak to about the payment of your invoices. Have a copy of the invoice in front of you. Take a couple of deep breaths and make sure you are sitting or standing confidently.

Have a clear idea of what you policy is. Make sure you know:

- Invoice number
- Invoice date
- Invoice amount
- Payment terms
- How many days extra credit you are prepared to give above your stated terms
- The number of days from invoice date after which you will charge interest or take further action
- Who you need to talk to who is responsible for bill payment

conversation

"Hi, my name is name, and I am the debt collection manager for company name. It has come to my attention that invoice number for £££, which we sent you on dd/mm/yyyy, remains unpaid and is overdue.

Please would you tell me when we can expect payment?"

Action 1

→ If the answer is a specific date in the coming week or two make a note of the date and who you spoke to. Thank them. Phone 2 days before that date, quote that you have been promised payment and check that your payment is in the next payment run.

→ If the answer is no payment is planned yet your response should be:

"Are there any problems with the work that has been carried out?"

Action 2

→ If the answer is yes, there are problems that are delaying payment find out who you need to talk to, to sort out any issues. Get them sorted. Then return to Action 1 and go through the same process again but make it clear that as far as you are aware there are no further problems, which should delay payment.

➜ If there are no problems:

"In that case payment of our invoice is due. Under the terms of our contract with you payment is due number of days from invoice date. Is there any reason why our invoice will not be included in your next payment run?"

Action 3

➜ If the answer is no, payment will be included in the next run, find out when that is, and thank them. Phone 2 days before that date, quote that you have been promised payment and check that your payment is in the next payment run.

➜ If the answer is that it will not be in the next payment run:

"As there is no problem with the work we have undertaken and as our invoice is overdue, I have to tell you what our policy is with late payers.

If you do not pay our bill within days from invoice date, we will charge you interest as allowed by the Late Payment of Commercial Debts (Interest) Act 1998. We will charge that rate of interest from the date of our bill to the date you pay even if we have to take court proceedings to recover the amount you owe.

If the invoice remains unpaid after days from invoice date, we will refer the matter to our legal team. If we take proceedings against you because you do not pay our bills, we will ask the court to order you to pay all of the costs we incur in those proceedings"

the science of debt collecting

the four step plan

1. Tell your customers what to expect

    If you don't do so already, make sure you send
    out sales order confirmations to any customers
    who have ordered goods or services from you.
    Take this opportunity to clarify what has been
    agreed.

2. Don't give credit as a matter of course

    If you are going to give credit make sure there is
    a business case for doing so and credit check
    customers to ensure you have the best chance of
    getting paid.

3. Invoice promptly

    Invoice for goods/services as quickly as you can
    after they have been delivered.

4. Have a debt collection policy and follow it
    rigorously when debts become due.

learning and action steps

Don't forget to fill this section – it can make a real difference to how much you learn from the workbook and how useful it is in helping you master your business finances.

Actions I will start doing   Importance Date

Actions I will stop doing   Importance Date

behaviour change log

Today's date _____

Review Date Issues	Reviewed	Outstanding
Tomorrow		
1 week		
1 month		
3 months		

getting third party finance

introduction – how to get finance

After you have reviewed your pricing and debt collection policies it may be that you still need to go to third parties for finance.

In fact, many businesses, particularly if they are growing, will need extra cash flow to fund their plans.

For the best chance of success you need to be prepared to build a case for the financing and show clearly what the money will be used for with a payment schedule of how you plan to repay it.

It will almost certainly help you if you can get professional help from your accountant in preparing the figures you will need, to prove you are a sound investment.

focus

This section's focus is on getting third party funding and we're going to cover:

➜ Why you might need the funding

➜ How to decide which type of funding is best for your need

➜ The types of business funding available

objectives

After completing this section you will be able to:

➜ Understand the options for funding available to businesses

➜ Match your need for funding with the most appropriate source

why do you need the money?

The first thing you need to be very clear on is why exactly you need the money. There are various different types of funding available but some are more appropriate than others depending on the need.

It is worth saying here that in recent times it has become the norm for funding providers to request personal guarantees from customers. This protects them from the business not being able to repay the loan. So if you are looking for finance do not be surprised to be asked to guarantee it personally – even if you are a director. You may even find you have to put down personal assets, such as your house, as security.

is the need long or short term?

This is the first question you need to ask yourself because it will influence which type of funding is most cost effective for your need.

If you have a short term need for cash (just a couple of months) to tide you until a large customer invoice is paid or to buy stock that will be sold quickly, an overdraft is probably the cheapest and most effective way of getting finance.

If you have a long term need for cash the solutions are more numerous but the most appropriate one will still depend on why you need the money.

what do you need the money for?

The answer to this question will make a difference to which type of funding is most appropriate.

Purchase of fixed assets

The most appropriate form of finance for buying larger pieces of equipment or motor vehicles is generally asset finance. It is a vehicle specifically designed for these types of purchases, and because the finance is linked to the item bought is safer for the lender – meaning it can be cheaper for you.

There are many asset finance companies out there so don't feel you have to go to your bank. In fact, your bank will probably be the most expensive provider. If you shop around you will get the most competitive price.

Inherent cash flow requirement

Some business models require that money is consistently paid out a long time before the customer pays for the goods or services.

An example of this is the provision of temporary staff by a recruitment agency. The staff must be paid weekly but customers often to pay 30 or 60 days later.

If you need money to fund this type of cash flow gap factoring or invoice discounting may be appropriate.

→ Full factoring

This means that all customer invoices are assigned to the funding provider. The funding provider then allows you to 'drawdown' a proportion of the money owed to you by customers (typically 80%).

Because customers receive statements from the funding provider it is obvious that the debt is factored and, depending on your contract with them, the factoring company will often chase the debts.

This solution tends to be the most expensive form of debtor financing.

Factoring is a well-established practise and most of the high street banks have a factoring arm. But, as with asset finance your bank may not provide the best rates so shop around.

→ Full debtor book invoice discounting

Invoice discounting is a reduced service, and so is a cheaper form, of factoring. In this case you do the customer chasing and they will often not know that you are borrowing against their invoice.

As with full factoring you will be able to drawdown against the amount owed to you by customers.

➜ Selective invoice discounting

In the case of selective invoice discounting you assign specific customers or invoices to the funding provider and they allow you to drawdown a percentage of those invoices only.

This is a relatively new type of debtor funding and generally not available through the high street banks.

A general note about debtor financing:

Most providers will only offer this type of funding if the product or service you provide is straight forward and the amount owed to you by your customers is easy to determine without any contractual difficulty.

This means that if your service is complex and the client can argue about the amount they owe you at any one time, funding providers are unlikely to want to help you or the fees will excessive.

Also be aware that if your business has a particularly large customer you may fall foul of 'concentration'. This is where the funding provider will only allow you to drawdown a lower percentage of the outstanding debt for this customer, because they deem the situation to be riskier.

Funding business growth

Funding the growth of your business is the most challenging funding to get and requires a more rigid approach.

Unlike asset financing or invoice discounting where the funds are specifically loaned against assets, growth funding is more difficult for lenders to assess.

This is because the funds borrowed will be used to build future profitability, which by its very nature is difficult to predict.

This means you will need to build a very good, well-reasoned, case for the funder to want to back your business and this will need to be in the format of a business plan (see the business planning section).

They will look at the current financial position of the business and assess how likely it is that you will be able to meet the repayment requirements of the loan.

There are various types of funding which are suitable for growth projects:

→ Bank loans

Traditionally bank loans would have been the cheapest and easiest form of growth funding for business owners to obtain.

However, in recent times banks have become more and more reluctant to loan money to businesses.

Despite the government's Enterprise Guarantee Scheme where 75% of the loan is guaranteed by the government, banks are reluctant to lend unless the business proposition is easy to understand and relatively risk free.

In particular, businesses in certain industries will find it exceptionally hard to get loan funding even if the business itself is pretty robust.

Bank lending has also become a fairly long process, so if you need the money quickly a bank loan is probably not the route to go down.

➔ Crowd funding

Crowd funding is a relatively new form of business funding but is gathering momentum.

The idea behind crowd funding is that a large number of relatively small investors club together through sites such as Funding Circle to provide peer to peer lending.

You can decide how long you wish to borrow the money for and investors bid to lend you money. The more investors are interested in your business the lower the interest rate you will need to pay.

Once your business is approved by the site money can be available to you much more quickly than, say, bank funding.

➔ Equity funding

This type of funding is often not so desirable to business owners because it requires them to give up a share of their company to the investor.

As in Dragon's Den the investor will value your company and then decide how much they are prepared to invest and what proportion of the company they want in return.

For new or high growth/high risk companies this form of funding may be a very good way of getting much needed finance.

how to borrow money

the four step plan

1. Decide exactly what the money is for

    If you are not clear the exact reasons you need to obtain third party funding it will be difficult, if not impossible, for you to do so.

2. Know which type of finance is best for your situation

    Effectively matching the form of financing with your need for cash is the best way of ensuring a good match. So make sure you have examined the various forms of financing open to you before you approach your preferred option

3. Prepare well

    Before approaching any finance provider ensure you have rigorously prepared. If the finance provider requires a business plan (and many do) make sure it clearly demonstrates the need for the finance and the ability of the company to repay any loan.

    Be prepared to answer any questions about your businesses and its finances openly, honestly, and knowledgably. How about preparing a list of questions you fear to be asked and have a good answer ready should these questions be asked?

4. Don't be discouraged by a no

The first provider you go to may not offer you the finance but keep trying. If you need the cash your company's future may depend on getting it.

learning and action steps

Don't forget to fill this section – it can make a real difference to how much you learn from the workbook and how useful it is in helping you master your business finances.

Actions I will start doing   Importance   Date

Actions I will stop doing   Importance   Date

behaviour change log

Today's date _____

Review Date   Reviewed   Outstanding
Issues

Tomorrow

1 week

1 month

3 months

SECTION 4

FACTS EVERY BUSINESS OWNER SHOULD KNOW ABOUT THEIR BUSINESS

There are key pieces of financial information successful business owners know about their business.

Some of these pieces of information are generic to pretty much every business but others are specific to individual businesses and will often be affected by the business sector they are in.

We have covered some types of key information earlier in the workbook but this section consolidates what has been covered already with further key information you may find useful for your business.

To ensure you are not running your business blindfolded it is important that you know the key statistics affecting your business.

Once you know what information is important in your business it is then obvious you will want to know how to get this information – so we will be covering this aspect too.

key performance indicators

introduction – what are KPIs?

It is possible to gather so much information about your business that it is difficult to see clearly what is important and what is just fog.

Key Performance Indicators (KPIs) are those statistics about a business that, if monitored, will have the biggest impact on its success.

It can be useful here to break down the terms into their individual words:

➜ Key

Key means that any business (or area of a business) should only focus on a handful of pieces of data. If you have lots of performance indicators you run the risk of being swamped with information.

➜ Performance

We want to measure the performance of the business over a period of time so the data we are going to use shows measurable indications of improvements (or not) over time.

➜ Indicators

We are looking for indicators of performance not the War and Peace of how the level of performance has come about. This means we want simple flags.

focus

This section's focus is on the key performance indicators and we're going to cover:

➜ What generic key performance indicators are relevant to most companies

➜ What specific KPIs might be useful in your business

objectives

After completing this section you will:

➜ Know which KPIs would give you the best information to help you grow your business

financial KPIs

Key performance indicators are designed to highlight areas in the business, which have significant impact on its success. KPIs can be both financial and non-financial in nature and will differ from business to business. In most businesses it will be sufficient to use four or five KPIs to give a summary position of how well it is doing.

A KPI, when measured and controlled, can help a business maximise its performance. For this reason it is important to choose KPIs which are meaningful to your particular business.

A great way to show how KPIs are changing from one period to the next is to use graphs – think about how you can show the information in the best way for you to understand and interpret.

generic KPIs

Gross profit

Gross profit is the profit you make on your sales after the direct costs of producing those sales are deducted. The reason it is an important measure for most companies is that it is directly linked to sales.

Whether measured in absolute terms or as a % of sales, gross profit can give great insights into how a company is performing. For example, if the GP % is falling it could indicate that goods and services are being sold too cheaply or inefficiencies in production are creeping in.

Net profit

Net profit is a measure many businesses use because it is easily understood and is calculated as part of the regular management information.

Net profit is the profit once you have deducted cost of sales and overhead expenditure from turnover.

Debtor days

'Debtor days' is a calculation of how quickly customers pay invoices. This indicator is particularly useful when cash flow is tight but can, in any case, be an indicator of how quickly the company converts sales into cash.

The lower the number the better able you are to convert sales into cash.

To calculate debtor days divide the debtors figure in your balance sheet by annual turnover and multiply the answer by 365.

As well as the simple debtor days calculation you will also want to know exactly which customers owe you money and how much is outstanding.

You may find that certain customers are continually late in paying in which case you need to get on top of why this is and encourage them to pay more promptly.

Order intake

Order intake is a measure of the value of orders received in a week/month/quarter.

In any company, but particularly in companies which deal in long term projects, order intake is a useful measure of how effectively the business is at winning new business and its ability to grow in the future.

Top customers

It is important for any business to know which customers spend the most money with them. These customers are probably the most important for your company and will account for a disproportionately large share of your sales revenue.

It makes sense that you will wish to ensure that these customers are happy because to lose one of them will have the biggest impact on your business.

Also these are probably the types of customer you want to attract more of and so knowing who they are will help you to direct your marketing effort.

Top profit earners

Above we said that your top customers by sales are 'probably' your most important ones but there is a further piece of information you need about each of them – what is the profit they earn you?

Many businesses are over attracted to customers who give them large sales but at such low profits that these customers are actually damaging the business.

A well-known example of this phenomenon is the relationship some supermarkets have with their suppliers. The supermarkets require a large proportion of the supplier's goods or services but are only prepared to pay a small profit on top of the basic cost of the goods or services.

Although this is quite a specific example beware of customers who ask for discounts for quantity.

By understanding which customers are the most profitable you will be able direct marketing effort both to keeping existing customers happy, but also to finding profitable customers for future growth.

Your get out of bed rate

Your 'get out of bed rate' is the minimum amount you need to earn from a sale to make it worthwhile making the sale. It is most useful for companies who provide services rather than goods.

For many businesses this rate will be linked to their breakeven point. The breakeven point is when the gross profit from sales equals overhead expenditure. This will be the point at which the company is making neither a profit nor a loss – but at least you know the basic costs of running the business (including salaries) are covered.

You need to know this so you don't chase unprofitable work.

other KPIs that might be useful

Customer complaints

Measuring the number of customer complaints is a great way of gauging how successful the business is in meeting its commitments to its customers. If the number of complaints is further broken down by type of complaint focussed changes can be implemented.

Staff turnover

If a business is staff-orientated, particularly where there is a degree of training involved in getting staff up to speed, measuring staff turnover can be very useful. If staff turnover is high it may be that something serious is wrong either in recruitment, or staff management. It is important to recognise that if the problem continues new staff training becomes an ongoing expenditure rather than a one off.

Number of customers and sales per customer

The 'number of customers' and 'sales per customer' measures are particularly useful in retail. For many retailers getting customers through the door is a major problem. Once customers have been engaged the next focus will be on maximising the amount of money spent in the store by each customer.

monitoring your business

the four step plan

1. Decide what is important in your business

    Before you can decide which KPIs are useful in your business you need to be clear on what makes your business 'tick'. Because you will concentrate on improving what you measure, it is vital you know the right things to focus on.

2. Decide which measures fit with what is important

    There are many different measures you can choose from and sometimes the most effective measure is very specific to the industry you are in. For example, for an IFA the amount of funds they are managing for clients may be key to the income they earn.

    Choose carefully and don't assume that the more measures you have the better. Because we are talking about KEY measures 5 or 6 will probably be enough.

3. Understand what the measure is telling you

    Measuring something is all very well, but if you don't understand how the measure works and what changes in the results are telling you, you won't be able to take effective action to move the business forward

4. Get help if you need it

   Again, choosing KPIs for your business and building an effective monitoring system is a fairly specialised skill so if you don't know what you are doing it may be wise to seek help.

learning and action steps

Don't forget to fill this section – it can make a real difference to how much you learn from the workbook and how useful it is in helping you master your business finances.

Actions I will start doing   Importance   Date

Actions I will stop doing   Importance   Date

behaviour change log

Today's date _____

<u>Review Date</u>   <u>Reviewed</u>   <u>Outstanding</u>
Issues

Tomorrow

1 week

1 month

3 months

developing your information systems

introduction – getting information

Even the smallest business can have effective information systems to help the owner understand their financial position.

The key thing to realise is that understanding the drivers of your business's finances can be a powerful tool in moving forward towards your goals – whether business or personal.

By focussing on providing HMRC with the information it wants you are missing out on a real trick, because you probably already have systems which, if tweaked, can provide you with robust management information too.

This section is all about helping you to set up this system.

focus

This section's focus is on how to set up a system for getting the information you need to run your business effectively. It will cover:

→ What types of financial systems might help

→ How to set them up to give you the information you need

→ Where to get help

objectives

After completing this section you will:

→ Be able to set up an effective financial reporting system

factors to think about

what resources are available to you?

Before you can think about what system is best for your business you need to identify what resources are available to you.

By resources we mean:

Time

How much time is available in your business for providing financial information? The answer to this question will determine which systems you implement first and which will need to wait until you have more time resource.

People

This is linked to 'time' above. Many businesses, especially smaller ones, rely on the business owner to 'do' the books. This is rarely a sensible way forward in anything other than the short term, so if you are in this position think about who would do the figure work if you don't.

Even if you don't have the budget to hire an employed bookkeeper engaging an external bookkeeper will almost certainly be cheaper for the company than you, the business owner, doing the job yourself. After all only you can get the sales your business needs or provide the strategy for your company.

Also, don't forget your accountant should be able to help you to set up your information system.

If they are unable, or unwilling, to do so it may be worth engaging a management accountant who can help you get started.

Money

If you are limited by the amount of money you have to solve your information problem – and we suspect this will be the case – you need to spend your money wisely. An apparently cheap option may actually be the most expensive one because it causes extra costs to be incurred elsewhere.

Systems you already have available to you

When companies are first set up their finance systems are often focused on providing information to third parties – i.e. for doing VAT returns and year end accounts. However, this does not mean that the computer programs you already use cannot be adapted to give you more pro-active information.

Most off-the-shelf accounting programs will give you the ability to do at least basic management reporting and core data can often be downloaded into Excel for further analysis, without having to do major changes.

Many companies have time tracking systems which can be useful in providing great additional information to management about customer costs.

If you are in retail your till system may be able to provide a lot more information than you are currently getting – particularly if it has an in built stock accounting system.

how computer literate is the person who currently does the 'books'?

These days the most effective information systems use computers. The best solutions involve some kind of accounting package and use of a spreadsheet package such as Microsoft Excel.

If your 'bookkeeper' is not very computer literate, or is very fixed in their ways of working, you may find it difficult to make the changes you need.

Ideally the person responsible for providing regular financial information will have the following:

- A good working knowledge of an accounts package (Sage, Quickbooks, Xero etc.)
- A good working knowledge of Excel
- Training as a bookkeeper at some level

do you, the business owner, want access to the system?

Although it is not good use of a business owner's time to do the 'books' themselves many business owners like to have ready access to information. Whether you do or not will affect your choice of system.

For example, if you do want access whichever system you choose will probably need to be cloud based, or at least server based, so it can be accessed by more than one person.

what do you really want?

Once you have answered the questions above you need to ask yourself, which pieces of information you want on a regular basis to help you run your business. This will determine how you need to adapt your current systems to provide this information.

management information systems

Taking some specific KPIs from the KPI chapter of this workbook, the section below gives you some pointers as to how you can obtain the information you need within your own business.

Gross and Net Profit

If you are using an excel spreadsheet to run your finances you will probably not have a very effective reporting system. Excel is great for manipulating data but less good as a data capture system.

All but the very smallest businesses will benefit from using a purpose built accountancy package.

Certainly if you are looking to employ a self-employed bookkeeper they will want to use such a package.

There are many to choose from and prices range from less than £20 per month for an online package, or £100 to buy a package for your in-house computer, to thousands of pounds.

The most popular providers of small business information packages include Sage, Xero, QuickBooks and Liquid Accounts. Some are cloud based only and others offer both cloud based and desktop based systems.

If you are clear on what information you want the package to provide, the decision on which package to choose should be pretty easy. If you have a bookkeeper it is often good to be led by them.

All packages will have an in-built profit and loss report that can provide your gross and net profit on a monthly basis – assuming the data entry is up to date! However, this report can be modified to give further information on sales and costs to help you monitor what is going on. It is just a case of setting the package up properly from the outset.

Again your accountant should be able to help with this.

Debtor days

Any accountancy package should be able to give you the information you need to calculate your debtor days.

Each will have a 'debtors' ledger' which lists any unpaid customer invoices and will tell you what your sales are.

Order Intake

This is not something your accounting package will be able to tell you, because until the order is invoiced there is nowhere for this information to be captured.

Many companies, including smaller ones, have developed great systems to help them to understand how potential customers move along the timeline from first meeting to quote to order to sales.

And there are off the shelf CRM packages out there to help you to manage this information.

However, if you don't want to go down that route having a simple Excel workbook where orders are recorded as they come in will help you to understand how effective your selling is.

Top customers

Again most accounting packages can tell you how much you have invoiced individual customers in a particular period and many have a simple report you can run to list your customers in value order.

Top profit earners

Finding out which of your customers are most profitable is more of a challenge than tracking sales, because you also need to be able to track customer specific costs.

Again some accounting packages have built in 'project accounting' systems that are able to attach costs to particular customers and/or products/services.

If you are in retail your till system may well be able to record your stock items in terms both of sales price and cost price. If you have not already explored using this facility it would certainly be advisable to do so, because you will be able to run very quick reports on which products are the most profitable for you.

However, if you don't have any systems already to hand you may be able to set up your own system using Excel.

➜ Time recording

For companies who sell time (consultants, IT support, the professions etc.) it is useful to capture the time staff spend on each client. There are many time recording systems available at different price points.

For the system to be effective ALL staff should record ALL their time, but it does not need to be to the second. Half hour slots are often adequate.

Each customer should have its own booking code, and you will need some non-customer time codes such as holiday, sickness, meetings, training etc.

At the end of the month you should be able to run a time log showing who worked on which customers and for how long.

By multiplying the time spent on a particular customer by the cost rate for the employees who did the work, you will know the time cost to you of servicing that customer.

If you then add on out-of-pocket expenses such as mileage, materials and other purchases you will have the full cost of sales.

Compare that with the income received and you have the customer profitability.

➜ Cost recording

Keeping a track of purchases made specifically for particular customers/projects should be relatively straight forward in a small company.

The key is to have a 'collection point' for each cost, which could be a tab on an excel spreadsheet or a separate code in your nominal ledger.

For larger companies it is well worth setting up 'project accounting', if your accounting package allows it, because it means that the cost can be assigned to a customer/project at the time the purchase invoice/expense is put into the accounting system.

Your get out of bed rate

To really get to grips with what this rate is you need to have a clear idea of the expected overhead costs for the coming year. So using your forecasted overheads is the best place to start.

The reason you want to use your future overhead spend as a starting point is that you will be using this rate to assess future sales – using a rate based on what has happened in the past will not necessarily lead you to the correct conclusions going forward.

However, if you don't have an idea of future overhead spend at least using last year's spend will give you a place to start.

Again your accounting package will be able to give you this information.

Once you know your overheads you know the minimum profit you need to earn in a year to survive. Add to this a percentage for profit and you will have the gross profit you want to earn.

For service companies dividing this amount by the number of hours staff are available to work on client work and you have your hourly 'get out of bed' rate.

Customer complaints

Again this is not a measure for which data is available from your accountancy programme. However, it should be an easy measure to track manually.

The key thing is to make it as easy as possible for customers who need to complain to do so and for staff to record when they do.

A complaints log in the form of an excel workbook accessible by everyone (or even a written log if that is easiest) should have space for the date, the name of the client, the nature of the complaint, who resolved it and how was it resolved.

In particular, it is important that unresolved complaints are tracked.

Staff turnover

This is another statistic which cannot be provided by the accounts system but which should be easy to track using an excel spreadsheet.

By listing each member of staff and noting their start and end dates of employment it is easy to monitor staff turnover rates.

Number of customers and sales per customer

As this generally relates to retail, till systems will generally record this information as a matter of course. They should be able to record the number of individual items a customer bought, and their value, as well as the total number of individual customers in a day.

From this retailers should be also able to run reports to give detailed information on which products are the best sellers – another useful statistic.

getting the information you need

the four step plan

1. Look at your existing systems

   It is not always necessary to get new systems to solve the information gathering problem. You may already have systems that you bought for a different purpose but can help with producing your KPIs.

2. Be clear what you are prepared to invest

   Optimising your management information is likely to cost some time and/or money so it is important to understand what your budget for both is. It may be that you need to implement the changes in stages rather than all at once, so look at the most important measures first.

3. Prepare well

   Don't just dive in head first. Planning the system changes will increase the likelihood of a stress free implementation.

4. Get help if you need it

   If you are not knowledgeable about accounting systems let someone who is run the show.

learning and action steps

Don't forget to fill this section – it can make a real difference to how much you learn from the workbook and how useful it is in helping you master your business finances.

Actions I will start doing   Importance Date

Actions I will stop doing   Importance Date

behaviour change log

Today's date _____

Review Date Issues	Reviewed	Outstanding
Tomorrow		
1 week		
1 month		
3 months		

and in the end...

Businesses exist to make money for their owners.

Many small businesses do not make money and the reason is often that the business owners are not financially savvy enough to make the right decisions for their businesses. However, until these businesses are able to stand on their own feet financially they will act as a net reducer to the wealth of their owners rather than a net enhancer.

Other small businesses are making money, but perhaps not at the levels the business owner feels is enough for the effort involved. Again, a focus on financial areas can help establish where changes can be made to make the business more profitable.

So, if businesses exist to make money for their owners, and a greater understanding business finances can help the business owners to create more wealth, my hope is that this book will aid business owners along their path to prosperity.

After all, running your own business is stressful enough without trying to do it without all the information you need to do it successfully.

a final note from fiona

This workbook is not designed to be read just once and then put on a bookshelf to gather dust. Please do revisit your action and behaviour change logs at the end of each section, to track how your learning is helping move your business forward.

I hope you have found this workbook useful – if so please tell other business owners you know.

If you haven't found it useful because you have not understood it all, please let me know so I can make changes to future additions.

You can contact me at:
fiona@fionabevanfinancialmanagement.co.uk

43335562R00076

Made in the USA
Charleston, SC
21 June 2015